The Life
and Work
of...

Salvador Dali

Leonie Bennett

Heinemann Library
Chicago, Illinois

Library of Congress Cataloging-in-Publication Data:
Bennett, Leonie.
    Salvador Dali / Leonie Bennett.
      p. cm. -- (Life and work of--)
    Includes bibliographical references and index.
    ISBN 1-4034-5071-4 (library binding) -- ISBN 1-4034-5561-9 (pbk.)
    1. Dalì, Salvador, 1904---Juvenile literature. 2.
    Artists--Spain--Biography--Juvenile literature. I. Title.
    II. Series.

N7113.D3B46 2004
709'.2--dc22

                          2004014057

Printed and bound by South China Printing Company, China

08 07 06 05
10 9 8 7 6 5 4 3 2 1

Acknowledgments
The author and publishers are grateful to the following for permission to reproduce copyright material:
AKG/Daniel Frasnay p. 20; AKG/Schutze/Rodeman p. 26; Bettmann/Corbis pp. 4, 14, 18; Bridgeman Art Library/ Museum of Modern Art, New York/Salvador Dali, Gala-Salvador Dali Foundation, DACS, London 2004 p. 15; Bridgeman Art Library/Christie's Images, London, UK p. 17; Bridgeman Art Library/Victoria & Albert Museum, London/Salvador Dali, Gala-Salvador Dali Foundation, DACS, London 2004 p. 5; Bridgeman Art Library / Bibliotheque Litteraire Jacques Doucet, Paris/Archives Charmet/Man RayTrust/ADAGP,Paris and DACS, London 2004 p. 10; Corbis/Archivo Iconografico.S.A./Salvador Dali, Gala-Salvador Dali Foundation, DACS, London 2004 pp. 9, 11; Corbis / B.D.V p. 24; Corbis/Stephanie Maze/Salvador Dali, Gala-Salvador Dali Foundation, DACS, London 2004 pp. 22; Hulton Getty p. 16; Patrick and Beatrice Haggerty Museum of Art, Marquette University, Milwaukee, WI. Gift of Mr and Mrs Ira Haupt, 59.9. © 2003 Marquette University, All rights restricted. No part of this image may be reproduced without the written permission of Marquette University, Milwaukee, Wisconsin 53233, USA/Salvador Dali, Gala-Salvador Dali Foundation, DACS, London 2004 p. 27; Photo authorized by the Gala-Salvador Dali Foundation pp. 6, 8; Ronald Grant Archive p. 13; Salvador Dali, Gala-Salvador Dali Foundation/ DACS, London 2004 pp. 7, 21, 23, 25; Staatliche Museen zu Berlin – Preussischer Kulturbesitz Nationalgalerie p. 19;

Cover painting (*Atavistic Traces after the Rain*, 1934) reproduced with permission of The Art Archive/Salvado Dali, Gala-Salvador Dali Foundation, DACS, London 2004 and portrait of Dali reproduced with permission of Bettmann/Corbis.

Every effort has been made to contact copyright holders of any material reproduced in this book. Any omissions will be rectified in subsequent printings if notice is given to the publisher.

Contents

Any words appearing in the text in bold, **like this**, are explained in the Glossary.

Who was Salvador Dali?

Salvador Dali was a Spanish artist. He painted strange, dream-like pictures. He was famous because of the way he looked and acted as well as for his works of art.

Salvador made objects and jewelry.
He even made films and furniture.
This is a sofa that looks like the lips
of a woman.

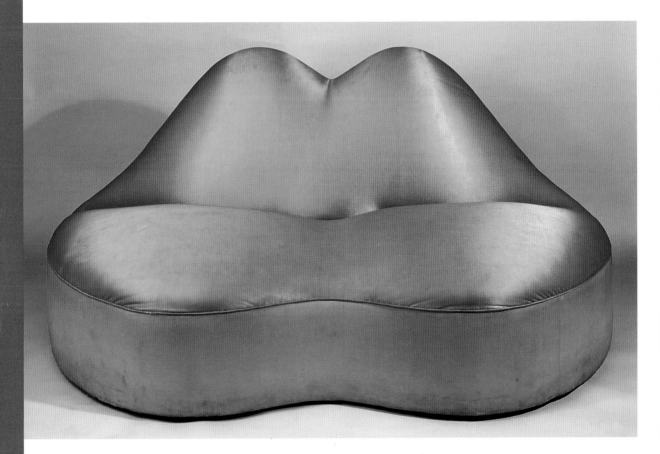

Mae West Lips Sofa, 1936–37

5

Early Years

Salvador was born on May 11, 1904, in Figueres, Spain. His father was a **lawyer**. Salvador was very spoiled. He didn't like school and often got into trouble.

Salvador always wanted to be a painter. He would draw pictures of his family at their vacation home by the beach.

The Dali family at their beachfront home, about 1918

Student Days

When he was seventeen, Salvador went to art school in **Madrid**. He was **rebellious** and often argued with his teachers. He liked going back to Figueres to visit his family. Here he is with his sister.

He often painted his father and his sister. His sister was the **model** for this picture. The **realistic style** is very different from his later paintings.

Figure at a Window, 1925

In Paris

In 1926, Salvador went to Paris. He joined a group of artists who called themselves **surrealists**. They made art that was more like dreams than like real life. Salvador is in the center of this photo.

Salvador was **expelled** from art school in **Madrid** because he caused trouble. In Paris he met a Russian girl called Gala. She became his **model** and then his wife.

The Angelus of Gala, 1935

The Film-maker

Salvador made **surrealist** films. The films had no story. Strange things happened, like they do in dreams. The films made some people angry. One **audience** threw ink at the cinema screen.

This is a picture from one of Salvador's films. Ants are crawling on a man's hand. How would you feel if you were watching this film?

From *An Andalusian Dog*, 1929

Making Strange Paintings

Salvador's father did not like his work. He would not speak to Salvador. Salvador and Gala went to live in a fishing hut in a village near Figueres.

Salvador used the **landscape** of Spain in his paintings. But things did not look as they do in real life. The watches in this picture look soft, like melted cheese.

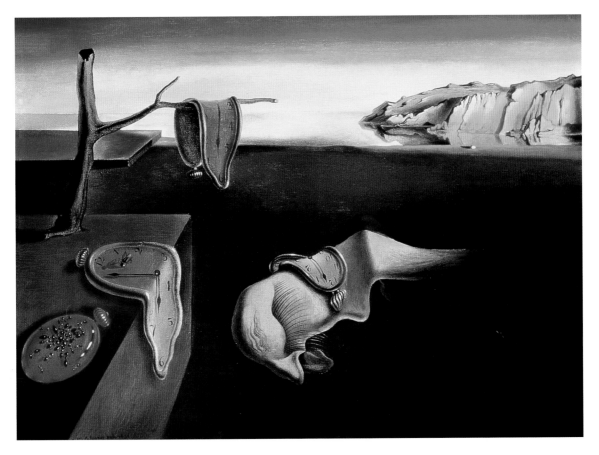

The Persistence of Memory, 1931

Making Strange Objects

Salvador collected all kinds of things. They gave him ideas for his art. The **surrealists** often made art from ordinary objects. They used them in surprising ways. Here Salvador is wearing an animal skull as a hat.

Salvador enjoyed putting together things that do not usually go together. This is his famous *Lobster Telephone*.

Lobster Telephone, 1936

In America

In 1940 Salvador went to America. The Americans were amazed by the things he did and made. Here he is with Gala at a party at their home.

Many rich people asked Salvador to paint **portraits** of them. This woman has a **brooch** like a tree on her chest. Salvador has also painted a rock and a forest. He has made them look like the woman.

Portrait of Isabel Styler-Tas, 1945

Being Famous

Salvador wanted to be a **celebrity**. He always tried to draw attention to himself. He had a big moustache that curled up at the ends. Many people thought he was crazy.

Salvador also made strange jewelry. These lips are made of rubies and gold. The teeth are made of pearls. You can wear it as a **brooch**.

Ruby Lips, 1949

A Theater-Museum

The people of Figueres were proud of Salvador. In 1974 they turned an old theater into a Dali museum. Many of his paintings and objects were shown there.

Salvador painted an amazing picture on one of the ceilings in the museum. He also made this elephant. It is called *The Space Elephant* and is made of gold and **precious stones**.

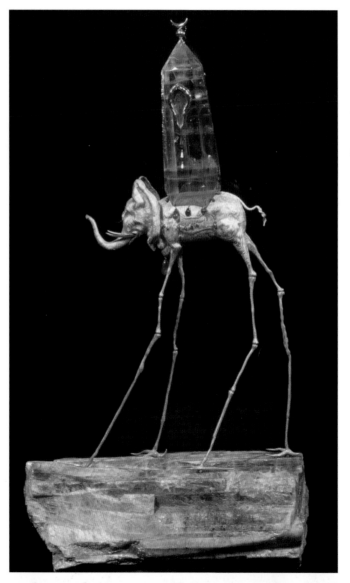

The Space Elephant, 1980

23

Alone in a Castle

In 1982 Gala died. This made Salvador very sad. He lived in a castle at Pubol, near Figueres, on his own.

Salvador often gave his works strange titles. This is a **still life** that is moving. It is called *Living Still Life*. He called another painting *Fried Eggs on the Plate Without the Plate*.

Living Still Life, 1956

Dali Dies

After a fire in the castle, Salvador went to live in the tower of the Figueres theater-museum. He did not paint much anymore. He was 84 years old when he died in 1989.

When Salvador died, he left everything he owned to the Spanish government. But you can see his work in museums around the world. This painting is Milwaukee, Wisconsin.

Madonna of Port Lligat, 1949

Timeline

1904   Salvador Dali is born in Figueres, Spain, on May 11.

1914–18   World War I takes place.

1918   Salvador draws a picture of his family at their beachfront home.

            Salvador's first public **exhibition** is held in Figueres.

1921   Salvador goes to art school in **Madrid**.

1925   Salvador paints his sister in *Figure at a Window*.

1926   Salvador goes to Paris for the first time. He visits Picasso.
            Salvador is **expelled** from the art school in Madrid.

1929   Salvador meets Gala Eluard.

            Salvador makes his first film with Luis Buñuel, *An Andalusian Dog*.

1930   Salvador and Luis Buñuel make make another film, *Age of Gold*.

1931   Salvador paints *The Persistence of Memory*.

1932   The first **surrealist** exhibition takes place in America.

1934   Salvador and Gala get married.

1935   Salvador paints *The Angelus of Gala*.

1936   The **Civil War** begins in Spain.
            Salvador makes the *Lobster Telephone*.
            Salvador makes the *Mae West Lips Sofa*.

1939   Salvador is expelled from the surrealist group for his **political** views. The Spanish Civil War ends. World War II begins.

1940	Salvador and Gala go to America to get away from the war.
1942	Salvador writes his **autobiography**, *The Secret Life of Salvador Dali*. He makes most of it up.
1945	World War II ends. Salvador paints **Portrait** *of Isabel Styler-Tas*.
1948	Salvador and Gala return to Spain.
1949	Salvador paints *Madonna of Port Lligat* and makes jewelry such as *Ruby Lips*.
1956	Salvador paints *Living Still Life*.
1974	The theater-museum of Dali's life and work opens in Figueres.
1980	Salvador makes *The Space Elephant*.
1982	Gala dies at Pubol castle.
1983	Salvador completes his last painting.
1989	Salvador dies in Figueres on January 23. He is buried in the **crypt** of the theater-museum.

Glossary

audience   people who watch a film or play

autobiography   story of someone's life, told by that person

brooch   piece of jewelry that pins on

celebrity   famous person

civil war   war between people of the same country

crypt   underground room

exhibition   show of art for the public

expelled   forced to leave a school or college

landscape   the countryside

lawyer   person who helps people understand the law

Madrid   capital city of Spain

model   person who an artist paints or draws

political   to do with the way the country is run

portrait   picture of a person

precious stone   stone like a diamond that is very valuable

realistic   like real life

rebellious   not wanting to do what you are told

still life   painting of a group of objects, such as a bowl of fruit on a table

style   the way something looks or is done

surrealist   artist who does work that is dream-like, using objects in an unexpected way

Find Out More

Paintings and sculptures to see

Painting. *Oedipus Complex*. 1930. San Francisco Museum of Modern Art.

Painting. *The Persistence of Memory*. 1931. The Museum of Modern Art, New York.

Painting. *The Dream*. 1931. The Cleveland Museum of Art.

Sculpture. *Aphrodisiac Telephone*. 1938. The Minneapolis Institute of Arts.

Painting. *Old Age, Adolescence, Infancy (The Three Ages)*. 1940. Salvador Dali Museum, St. Petersburg, Florida.

Books to read

Anna Obiols et al. *Dali and the Path of Dreams*. London UK: Frances Lincoln, 2004.

Angela Wenzel. *Adventures in Art: The Mad, Mad, Mad World of Salvador Dali*. New York: Prestel Publishing, 2003.

Robert Anderson. *Salvador Dali*. New York: Scholastic, Franklin Watts, 2002.

Index